Nature is Everything

SEEDS OF WISDOM FOR THE MATURING INTELLECT – BOOK ONE

By Nelunika Gunawardena Rajapakse

Copyright

Philosophical Wisdom

Rooted in LOVE

In homage to my parents
Dionicious and Mildred Gunawardena

Let us sow the seeds of culture
In our children's hearts from the very beginning

So that they may grow to love, to wonder, and to marvel
At the ever unfolding story—the wisdom of humanity

Let their love be unconditional
So it may permeate the world in its totality

Let us inspire our children to understand, and to cherish
The deeper meaning of their love
For they are the keepers of social integrity

Let us, hence, nourish their intellects
With unbounded opportunity

To appreciate the interdependent realities…
The expressions of the human spirit

Which leave behind their everlasting imprints
Called, culture and diversity

Nelunika Gunawardena Rajapakse

Dedication

This is a Special Tribute

In Reverence to My Beloved Parents

Dionicious and Mildred Gunawardena

who lived to epitomize

the wisdom of loving kindness and compassion

towards all beings and forms

who traversed their paths on Earth,

throughout their lifetimes.

Foreword

This book is a 'Seeds of Wisdom for The Maturing Intellect' presentation for the children of humanity—aged six years and above—who deserve to be immersed with knowledge at the base of TRUTH. Our temporal experience is the product of sensory impressions and associated emotive and cognitive thought processes. However, when a child matures with intellectual curiosity and imaginative reasoning, grounded upon his experiential journey of life, it is time that his human tendencies—marked with unique individual sensitivities—are matched with phase and time appropriate opportunity, to penetrate the depths of knowledge.

To nurture the nature of a child, succinctly said, is to support him in light of his unique psychophysical characteristics—in adherence to his particular developmental phase.

There are four formative developmental periods, though, to keep in mind. These range from conception through twenty-four years of age.

The following is an outline of the transformational phases of human metamorphic development—from childhood to adulthood:

- The most impressionable, tender being of 0—6 years

- The maturing personality of 6—12 years (endowed with a curious imagination and a reasoning intellect to understand his world)

- The adolescent of 12—18 years (a sensitive and vulnerable worldling in formation and transformation under the influence of active hormones)

- The young adult of 18—24 years (yearning to stabilize his twofold human purpose—for his own sake, and for the world at large)

In consideration of the fact that a maturing personality of six years and above is a curious explorer of his greater world—the infinite universe, the more he grows to understand Nature's inner workings, the more passionate he may become about LIFE.

Foreword continued

The happy consequence of nurturing the human body, mind (intellect), and spirit—phase appropriately—is to witness a fulfilled, maturing personality imbued with a wholesome outlook on life. He will cherish each breath of his human condition with appreciation and admiration, wonder and awe, and finally, gratitude for all that is—realizing that he is an integral microcosmic aspect of the macrocosmic whole, receiving from, and returning LOVE with reciprocity to the universe.

As you may note, the content of this book calls for investigative and reflective attention. The propitious transmission of seeds of knowledge, while there is demonstrated readiness to embrace information, is the key point to make.

Therefore, pointers to in-depth understanding, exploration, and discovery of life in the universe must take place in the form of **an unfolding story of LIFE;** it must begin from a discernible point in history. Along this process of discovery—as to who we are, and what we are—by means of this beautiful unfolding story of LIFE, the very experience of 'living to learn' or 'learning to live' must be grounded upon the base or bedrock of morality, as the compassionate, underpinning wisdom of the universe.

Differently expressed, the nature of our universe at its core, or ground, epitomizes the ultimate wisdom or TRUTH in action—as compassionate healing of the highest order; it upholds the principles of EQUALITY and RECIPROCITY in consideration of all beings and forms that wish for their happiness. The manifest universe becomes a field of eternal redemption—placing moral responsibility upon the exercise of FREEDOM—in response to the actions of human FREE WILL.

This is where the story must begin; the fusion of the four wondrous energies of resistance, cohesion, motion, and transmutation interactively bring forth all magical sensory phenomena that we—as terrestrial beings or forms—experience in the luminous emptiness of SPACE.

All in all, it is my fervent hope that this book, upon your reading and its completion, will arouse deeper curiosity, appreciation, and admiration for all that we experience as the wondrous nature of LIFE!

Table of Contents

Essence, Energy, and Matter

Appreciating the Trinity of Being

Nature's Essence Body
1

Our human reality is composed of two dimensions—these exist because of each other; they are two aspects of one whole, called **consciousness.**

The two dimensions of consciousness are namely,

the original unconditioned SELF-NATURE of 'suchness'—as the 'ultimate' dimension

and the reality of relativity—through interconnectedness—as the relative dimension of our human experience.

Two Interactively Inseparable Realities
2

The original reality—also called primordial nature—is a field of infinite possibilities. It is unborn and unconditioned. What exists there is 'pure essence', as potential for <u>all</u> possibilities—by way of life-events—called phenomena. Therefore, it may be looked upon as the **womb** of <u>all</u> phenomena.

The relative dimension—of interrelated, co-emergent, and coexistent phenomena—is the reality of human experience. It is the marvelous psychophysical display of an interactive energy spectrum.

Nature's Energy Body
3

Nature's energy body is the precursor to all formations, in terms of material phenomena.

Hence, energy is the interface between **essence—as potential—** and **matter.** Energy partakes in both of these fields.

Energy evolves from the body of essence; it is eternal and indestructible.

Energy may only be transformed.

In light of this fact, every form of energy obeys the universal law of conservation, which affirms that energy can neither be created, nor destroyed.

Energy as the Four Forces of the Universe
4

Energy arises as forces of the universe.

In a conventional sense, there are four fundamentally interactive forces in the universe—ranging from the largest to the smallest magnitude of influence, as a particular field of energy.

They are as follows:

- **Gravitational Force**

- **Electromagnetic Force**

- **Strong Nuclear Force**

- **Weak Nuclear Force**

Gravitational Force
5

The gravitational force is a continuous field of influence across the infinite expanses of the universe—however, it is the weakest of the four forces. All objects—with mass, energy, and momentum—are subject to the pull or force of gravity, which only attracts, but does not repel.

Gravitation affects the large-scale scheme or structure of the universe; it cannot be absorbed, transformed, or shielded.

Electromagnetic Force
6

The electromagnetic force is a discreet quantum field (a spatially localized body of energy, as a packet of energy)—of electromagnetic energy-absorption, emission, and interaction—affecting macrocosmic phenomena across the infinite expanses of the universe.

It is the stronger force than that of gravity that acts between electrically charged particles; it is responsible for macroscopic events such as lightening and chemical bonding—at the atomic level.

Strong Nuclear Force
7

The strong nuclear force is a discreet quantum field of influence within a subatomic distance—responsible for binding atomic nuclei.

Weak Nuclear Force
8

The weak nuclear force is a discreet quantum field of influence within a subatomic distance—acting upon the nuclei and responsible for radioactive decay.

Conventional Study of Nature's Body of Energy
9

The four forces of the universe interactively project the electromagnetic spectrum that, in turn, manifests the physical attributes of matter in terms of the following:

- light and radiation other than heat

- heat

- sound

- magnetism

- electricity

- mechanics of motion

The study of the above physical properties of matter and their dynamic interaction is known as PHYSICS.

Nature's Body of Matter
10

Nature's body of matter is a projection or construction of mind—based upon sensory inputs.

This process is psychophysical by nature. It is the magical display of electromagnetic energy at work, creating the illusion of space and time.

Matter, from a deeper perspective of reality, is the very union of four interactively engaged, sublime energies—discernible to the mind alone—resistance, cohesion, motion, and transmutation infiltrated and surrounded by space.

These forces may only be experienced and understood when they coalesce infinitely to form material substances—as atoms and molecules.

Matter as Four States
11

In an experiential, physical sense, matter exists in four states—as solid, liquid, gaseous, and plasma—always present with the four interactive, sublime energies of resistance, cohesion, transmutation, and motion.

The qualities noted above are symbolized by the aggregate material energies of earth, water, fire, and air that, together, are responsible for bringing forth the world of substances—penetrated and surrounded by space.

The four material energies—as aggregates of each other—are incessantly interactive and regarded as the fundamental constituents of the world of sensory phenomena, called experience.

Our Material World of Substances
12

There are a little over one hundred known basic chemical elements, or substances, in the universe, and ninety-eight are found to occur naturally on Earth.

They cannot be broken down or inter-converted into simpler substances.

These are conventionally looked upon as the primary constituents of matter.

Each element is a chemical substance that consists of atoms—composed of the same number of protons in their atomic nuclei.

Each substance is conventionally distinguished by its atomic number that defines the number of protons in the nuclei of its atoms.

The Great Union
13

All elements in the universe assume the solid, liquid, gaseous, or plasma states of matter, contingent upon **the nature of the union** of the four universal energies.

They are proportionately combined—by way of multiples of units—of earth (of resistance), water (of cohesion), air (of motion), and fire (of transmutation).

In our spacio-temporal world, the four abstract universal energies are understood only in the form of substances, looked upon as the great elements—of earth, water, air, and fire.

Interestingly, ancient wisdom states thus:

While every material substance is a proportionate combination of the four energies—in terms of units of energy, and their multiples—one of the four energies is reduced to one unit, in every given substance.

Nature's Universal Energies
14

Every known material substance in the universe, as aforementioned, is a tight embrace of the four universal energies or qualities—surrounded and infiltrated by space—differing uniquely in combination and proportion from another.

Earth symbolizes resistance—**rigidity**—as hardening or softening.

Water symbolizes cohesion—**humidity**—as flowing or pasting.

Air symbolizes motion—**movement or motility**—as expanding or contracting.

Fire symbolizes transmutation—**erratic light**—as color diffusion, and **warmth,** as heating or cooling.

Space symbolizes empty essence—infiltrating and surrounding all phenomena of sensory perception.

Our Empirical World
15

Every atom, therefore, represents a particular basic element, or chemical substance—as a sensory phenomenon—composed of the four aforementioned, wondrous material energies.

Our empirical world of convention, we continue to experience, is none other than being the intermingling of these four abstract material energies—ceaselessly uniting and separating—to project the changing world of substances.

Nature's Quality of Resistance

Appreciating the Great Element Earth, in Nature

Characteristics: to Harden and to Soften

Solidity Is Our Ground
16

Nature is the wonder of solidity.

Solidity is the ground of our home, the Earth.

The Earth—as the base of solidity and rigidity—is conceptualized in terms of the geometric shape, named 'square'.

The square symbolizes grounded-ness and immobility.

Earth, Our Home Sweet Home!
17

The Earth is home to everyone and everything.

All things, as life-events, are possible because of Earth, our great mother of unconditional LOVE and resistance.

Resistance is strength!

Earth, Our Mother of Unconditional LOVE
18

Earth is 'mother' to all children on our planet—in name, form, and being.

It symbolizes solidity and resistance.

All physical, physiological, and psychological processes bear earth's nature of solidity and resistance.

All structures—both physical and physiological—are none other than earth's nature of solidity and resistance at work.

Coarse, Gross Earth
19

The abstract earth element is the coarsest and grossest of all <u>four</u> material energies of wondrous nature—surrounded and infiltrated by space—as enumerated below.

- earth (of resistance)

- water (of cohesion)

- air (of motion)

- fire (of transmutation)

- space (of spaciousness, as empty essence)

The four energies, together, in engagement with each other, pervade LIFE from the densest to the subtlest states—or levels of being—permeated by all transcending and unconditioned space, of course.

Earth, the Ground of Being
20

Earth, as we continue to experience, is our mother—the unfailing protector, conserver, and nurturer of LIFE—abounded with unconditional LOVE and compassion to all of being.

It is the incubator and preserver of all that exists, nurturing every breath of life to the best and fullest of its own capacity—when conditions deem proper.

It is the base or foundation upon which any, or all, of transformation is made possible.

After all, where would life evolve, if not for Earth—our spacio-temporal ground of being?

Earth, Our Home of Equal LOVE
21

Earth is home of equal LOVE to all facets of being that intersect or converge to compose life—in the grand scheme of inter-being, called existence.

It is the breeding ground of infinite potential.

Earth is our mother that serves to epitomize non-discrimination.

It bears the unbounded and unparalleled energy of benevolence and equanimity.

Earth, the Container, and Contained
22

Earth is both 'the container and contained' of nourishment for all of 'being and form'—by way of supple matter.

Its charitable action in terms of 'giving and receiving' to nurture life and its evolution—in myriad ways, means, and forms—is to be witnessed through every breath of being.

Earth's sublime presence may be envisioned by its color, named 'harvest yellow', that exemplifies warmth and fertility.

Earth's Force of Gravity
23

Earth is our mother dwelling where all things settle, magnetized by its LOVE—as **the force of gravity.**

That being the case, all things settle according to their weight; the lighter the composition of elements, the closer it will be to the Earth's surface; the heavier the composition, the closer it will be to the core of the Earth.

Earth, a Reservoir
of Mineral Substances
24

Earth is a reservoir of mineral substances in eternal transformation influenced by the interactive and counteractive energies of water, wind, and fire.

The study of the Earth's structure—by way of substances, their formations, and their transformations—is conventionally known as GEOLOGY.

The investigative study of the nature of attractions, repulsions, and reactions between the substances, together, with their changes, compositions, and identifications, is conventionally known as CHEMISTRY.

Earth, Our Mother
of Warmth and Fertility
25

Mother Earth is the incubator and nurturer—of LIFE that evolves by natural selection.

Habitats and their flora and fauna find the cooperative conditions for their birth, evolution, preservation, and transformation because of mother Earth's sublime presence of wisdom and compassion. Earth's wisdom heals LIFE—grounded upon the principles of equality and reciprocity—through eternity.

The conventional perspective of investigation in regard to flora is known as BOTANY, while the study of fauna is termed ZOOLOGY.

The interactive study of both aspects is understood as BIOLOGY.

Earth's Order and Balance
26

Earth is our great mother—the conserver and preserver—of order and balance in existence, conventionally defined as ECOLOGY.

It balances and harmonizes all that exists with profound LOVE at its best, called **EQUALITY**—in keeping with the checks and balances of interdependent co-emergence, succinctly expressed as **co-existence and reciprocity.**

Earth's Wisdom and Compassion
27

Earth is our mother—never to be taken for granted—whose sublime presence of solidity and security calls for our unconditional respect and reverence towards it, with mindfulness.

Earth is our mother—of total **wisdom and compassion**—perpetually nurturing and giving to all facets of 'being and becoming' unobstructed by the diffusions of thought.

Earth is the epitome of LOVE!

Earth's Transcendent Qualities
28

Earth is our mother—of tolerance, acceptance, humility, forgiveness, and resilience—never repulsed by the follies of ignorance in relation to sentient kind, but relentlessly charitable, and unconditionally caring and compassionate, to all forms of life.

Mother Earth Balances the Equation, Called LIFE
29

In summation, one may say that Earth is our mother who checks and balances the great equation, called **'LIFE',** in collaboration with the three other indispensable and wondrous material energies— **water, air, and fire;** these together, in engagement with each other, manifest the world of substances, and thereby, all phenomena, infiltrated by all-pervading space!

Earth, as a Sensory Experience
30

The earth element symbolizes resistance and solidity.

It gives rise to the sense of smell.

Nature's Quality of Cohesion

Appreciating the Great Element of Water, in Nature

Characteristics: to Flow and to Paste

Nature, the Wonder of Fluidity
31

Nature is the wonder of fluidity.

Fluidity is the quality of flexibility, adaptability, or malleability.

Malleability is the propensity to be continuous—infiltrating or penetrating all things in existence.

Our very existence and its sustenance would not be possible without nature's wondrous energy of fluidity or liquidity.

Liquidity is the cohesive quality of water without which life cannot be sustained.

Water, the Second Aggregate Energy of Wondrous Nature
32

Water is the second aggregate of the four wondrous material energies, called the 'great elements'; these range from the coarsest to the subtlest by nature— looked upon as earth, water, fire, and air— permeated by space.

While they are aggregates of each other, they operate synergistically to create the sensory world of phenomena, or consciousness, in the emptiness of space.

Water, the Life-Sustainer
33

Water may be best described as cohesion.

It is the quality of wondrous nature's generosity that embraces, infiltrates, and surrounds.

Water signifies the life-sustaining quality of existence.

It epitomizes the unconditional love of nature towards all things that share the one breath of wisdom-compassion.

Water,
Its Nature of Transparency
34

Water is the cleanser, cooler, purifier, clarifier, and pacifier, for all of being.

It is the rescuing property of nature's selfless love.

Water means mirror wisdom; it sees through the eyes of all beings; it reflects compassion of inconceivable, unfathomable proportion.

Water's Resilience
35

Water is one of the four states of matter in which the particles are loosely held to roll over each other—both sideways and downwards—bringing forth nature's resilience or the cohesive quality of LOVE that embraces and surrounds.

Water signifies the wisdom of equality while it epitomizes the virtue of unconditional adaptation—as existence—taking the shape of the hollow that contains it!

Water, the Pacifier
36

Water pacifies the element of fire—when it is out of balance—in the physical, physiological, and psychological states of being.

All of the aforementioned states of being are ephemeral by nature; as realities of life-experience, they are processes that must be held in harmony and equilibrium with the support of the water element.

Water, however, operates in synchrony with the other three great material energies in order to make life possible, and sustainable.

Water is LIFE
37

Water is the source from which the moisture and succulence, the drips, and the oozes, in the physical universe—such as oil, milk, sap, and juice—come into being.

Water lies beneath all physiological functions— by way of life-blood and secretions.

It is also the pacifying quality in the psychology of our very being—expressed as temperament.

Water's Creative and Destructive Potential
38

Water inherently bears its creative and destructive potential.

When it is out of balance, water's ferocious nature can only be held under control by the element of air.

Water,
a Discrete Mover and Carver
39

Water is a discrete mover and carver by its very nature—bringing about erosion and the consequential contours and sculptures of the earth.

Water, in all of its forms—from solidity (as ice) to viscosity and vapor—is responsible for sculpting the earth, in cooperation with air and fire.

Water, the Harmonizer
40

Water, in an intrinsic sense, signifies resilience, cohesiveness, harmony, and malleability.

It epitomizes compassion through all of its manifestations in existence.

That being said, the ultimate human aspiration must be to transform passion into compassion.

Water Symbolized
41

Water is symbolized in terms of the geometric shape named sphere that signifies mobility and liquidity.

Water, in essence, means appearance without residue. It embodies the mirror like nature that characterizes the 'transparence' of being!

Water's symbolic color is white, which conveys purity and clarity.

Water
as a Sensory Experience
42

The water element gives rise to the sense of taste.

Nelunika Gunawardena Rajapakse

Nature's Quality of Motion

Photo credit: www.publicdomainpictures.net

Appreciating the Great Element of Air, in Nature

Characteristics: to Expand and to Contract

Nature,
the Wonder, of Mobility
43

Mobility is nature's wondrous ability for movement.

Movement or motion helps growth and transformation.

Growth and transformation is our very existence—as 'being and becoming'—from one moment to the next, in time.

Time ticks to move things forward.

All things in life are in motion—in the spacious wonder of space, itself!

Air,
the Breath of Life!
44

Air is our very breath of life; it is our life-giver.

Would there be existence in the absence of air, our vital energy?

Air is one of the four energies of wondrous nature. Swift air's very subtle density of particles enables it to move lightly in all directions, without obstruction.

It is, therefore, 'the mover' that helps to transform life from one state to another.

Air enables expansion and contraction.

Air, Life Giver and Mover of Our Temporal Body of Being
45

Air spontaneously operates to fulfill the primary purpose of its life-giving nature in the form of ten winds (inclusive of the secondary winds of sensory operation) within our material process of being.

They are as follows:

- **life-bearing wind energy**—its function is to maintain life; it gives rise to <u>the six secondary winds</u> which govern sensory operation and attention

- **equalizing fire-dwelling wind energy**—its function is to generate inner heat through yogic trance; it also aids digestion and metabolism

- **ascending wind energy**—it governs speech, absorption, and associated processes such as swallowing, burping, and spitting

- **descending wind energy**—its function is to control the three forms of elimination

- **all-pervading energy**—its main seat rests in the joints enabling movement, stretching and contracting the limbs, opening and closing the mouth and eyelids

Air, Life Giver and Mover of the Physical Universe
46

Essentially, the birth, existence, evolution, dissolution, and re-evolution of the physical universe becomes our experiential reality, primarily due to the wondrous element of air—upon which our sentient life-force rides—in cooperation with the three remaining abstract material energies.

Air, needless to say, is the progenitor of movement by which growth, advancement, and evolution, in every respect—physically, physiologically, and psychologically—is made possible.

Air is the precursor to all vacillations—as progressions and regressions—in life!

Air, Responsible for Growth and Transformation
47

Air causes growth and transformation in the vast and incomprehensible fabric of LIFE.

The cyclical order of air's activity—in collaboration with the three remaining wondrous energies permeated by space—is best known as the world of phenomena, or world of change.

Air spurs the mineral, vegetal, and animal kingdoms to interact, bringing about ecosystems rich in biodiversity and symbiotic interrelationships.

Air, the Mover and Carver
48

Air may be described as the swiftest mover and carver—bringing about erosion and the consequential contours and sculptures of the Earth, in cooperation with water and fire.

Air, on the other hand, is the very life-breath—of all beings and forms—that weaves the ceaseless rhythm of evolution.

Air,
the Epitome of Selflessness
49

Air epitomizes the qualities of unconditional love, empathy, equanimity, and <u>swift</u> compassion towards all of being.

Air—like the other sublime elements that compose wondrous nature within the vastness of all-pervading space—operates only in collaboration and cooperation with the three remaining wondrous energies, discerned through the world of substances as earth, water, and fire.

Air contains the creative and destructive potential of the universe; whatever the case might be, it epitomizes the ultimate truth of 'selflessness'.

Air's Creative and Destructive Potential
50

Air's pace of swiftness is an indication of its power to either pacify or to destroy.

When air picks up speed, beware!

When it brushes our skin with a gentle tingle, enjoy its caress!

Air Symbolized
51

The symbolic shape for air is the semi-circle; it signifies that it bears the characteristics of earth (rigidity) and water (malleability).

Its color is green; it denotes that earth's amber aura and water's blue hue—in fusion—bring about green.

Air
as a Sensory Experience
52

The air element gives rise to our sense of touch.

Nature's Quality of Transmutation

Photo credit: www.publicdomainpictures.net

Appreciating the Great Element of Fire, in Nature

Characteristics: to Heat and to Cool

The Wonder of Fire
53

Nature is 'the wonder of fire' that radiates heat.

Fire combusts, transmutes, and transforms life.

Life existence is born with fire, as heat!

Fire is the most erratic and restless form of nature's four wondrous material energies—earth, water, fire, and air.

The four wondrous energies interact to create our world of substances; as to whether a substance is in a solid state, liquid state, gaseous state, or a plasma state, is determined by the energy of heat or fire.

Abstract Energy of Fire
The Miracle beneath All of Life!
54

Abstract heat, being the most restless of the four energies, travels erratically from one substance to another. Along this process, its increase or decrease in a particular substance alters the state and nature of that substance. All physical disturbances—as we universally experience—are caused by the circulations of abstract heat.

Heat, thus, enters into substances and escapes from substances unceasingly throughout the spectrum of LIFE. In general, the catalyst beneath the migrations of all four energies—as a universal phenomenon—in and out of substances, is abstract heat.

A Survey of Heat's Activity in the Universe
55

The following is a brief survey of heat's activity in the universe:

- **Substances and their origin**

No substance comes into being without abstract heat. All substances utilize heat for their very existence.

- **Abstract heat, the agent of life and death**

The origination, preservation, cessation, and rejuvenation of life can only take place because of abstract heat. The excess or deficiency of this element causes the destruction of a material process.

- **Heat settles substances**

Heat is the chief mover of all physical phenomena; it is responsible for settling substances into the four states of matter—as solid, liquid, gaseous, and plasma.

- **Circulations of matter and energy**

The settled natures of substances disturbed and disrupted by excess heat causes circulations of matter and energy on Earth and throughout the universe.

- **Transformations in terms of states of matter**

The escape of heat from Earth to other bodies in space and the consequent loss of heat in the substances create converse reactions—as disturbances on our own planet.

In addition, heat's continual migration—from one state to another—is known to be the common reality. As such, states of matter transform incessantly—from earth to air, from air to earth, from water to air, from air to water, from fire to earth, air, and water, from earth, air, and water to fire.

- ## Chief mover of all phenomena

Fire or heat is the chief mover of all phenomena in the universe—physical, physiological, and psychological. No material being or process remains constant due to the changing presence—or absence—of heat from all aforementioned universal phenomena.

The Fire of Life
56

Can we ever imagine life without the combusting, transmuting nature of fire?

The catalyst beneath birth, evolution, preservation, and dissolution—not forgetting rebirth of phenomena—is fire.

The mind-generated fire element of every being sustains the equilibrium of its material life process under a constant temperature—regardless of atmospheric temperatures that can be higher or lower dependent upon the nature of its physical conditions.

Despite atmospheric interferences that persist, bombarding every life process—with the tendency to establish a temperature equal to it within a physical life system—it never succumbs to outside forces.

The only time when a body's temperature equals to a particular atmospheric temperature is when the mind no longer exists in a physical system—at death. The physical system, thus, quickly settles into the temperature of the atmosphere as a part of the environment.

Fire's Light of Life
57

Can we ever imagine life without light?

Light is the very reason beneath all of life.

Sentient sight is none else but light!

Light emanates from two sources—the sun and fire.

Our sentient experience is possible only within the visible light spectrum—that ranges between infrared and ultraviolet—of the electromagnetic spectrum.

Fire's Warmth or Heat of Life
58

Can we ever imagine life without warmth or heat?

Heat, as we continue to witness, spurs life into 'being and becoming' through four stages:

- from infancy to childhood

- childhood to youth

- youth to adulthood

- adulthood to decay

The same cyclic process takes place in the plant world—from a seed to a seedling, from a seedling to a plant, from a plant to a tree, and from a tree to its culmination—together as birth, death, and re-birth of phenomena, of course.

The heat of life ceaselessly re-kindles infinite cyclic material processes from birth, to death, to rebirth.

Heat, in essence, stimulates the growth of living beings to their prime and 'burns' them to death— soon to be transformed into a new material process.

Fire's Power of Transmission
59

Fire transmits light, heat, and sound in the universe.

Its wondrous nature is continually displayed in its intrinsic power—to create, and to destroy, simultaneously.

We call this transformation through combustion.

Fire, the Generator
60

Fire is the generator of all that is, called life.

Fire combusts and generates heat and light through space with the cooperative abstract element of air.

Fire is the radiant energy of the sun that sustains the waves and frequencies of the electro-magnetic spectrum.

The fire generated in the sun through circulations of its heat—to and from the neighboring planets and stars—is spontaneously radiated in all directions.

Thus, the circulation of heat keeps all spatial bodies in balance without setting them ablaze. They—not forgetting our planet Earth—are able to maintain a constant temperature due to these circulations of heat.

Fire, In and Out of Balance
61

Fire in balance is LIFE, itself!

Fire's potentially ferocious nature can be pacified with the element of water.

Fire—like the rest of the elements—when out of balance, is capable of destroying all of form.

Fire Pervades Mind and Matter
62

Fire is inherent in all that composes mind and matter.

It is reflected as **temperature** in everything that we feel and touch.

It is reflective of **temperament** when it relates to the mind.

Fire, the Catalyst of Change
63

Fire's transmuting energy pervades the whole of our universe—while it continually depicts life's cosmic dance of evolution and dissolution through incessant revolutions.

Transformation is the nature of LIFE; fire, to reiterate, is the catalyst beneath all of life, growth, and transformation.

Fire, Symbolized
64

The symbolic shape for fire is the triangle, which is indicative of an arrow soaring upward—symbolizing transmutation.

Its color is red that is illustrative of the aura of warmth.

Fire, as a Sensory Perception
65

The fire element gives rise to the sense of sight.

Nature's Quality of Luminous Emptiness

Photo credit: www.publicdomainpictures.net

Appreciating the Great Element of Space, All-Pervading, in Nature

The Womb of All Phenomena

The Wonder of Space, All-Pervading
66

Nature is the wonder, of all-pervading space.

Space is the field of infinite potential or limitless possibilities—also known as the womb of all phenomena in existence.

Phenomena are manifestations in life, understood as consciousness.

Life-events arise, abide, decline, dissolve, and re-emerge unceasingly in the openness of space.

Space is the play-field of wakefulness or interrelatedness—as presence, supreme—for the great dance of life.

Space Emanates Sound and Light
67

Life exists as the wakeful empty essence of sound and light—casting shadows of appearance and disappearance in the spacious wonder of space, itself!

Every vibration of energy is accompanied by sound; sound, in turn, is uniquely experienced in accordance with the particular configurations within the diversity of sentience.

The diffusions and differentiations of light bring to bear the colorful apparitional visions—or objects of sensory perception—by way of shape, form, and being.

Space, a Noumenon
68

Space is a noumenon—a thing as it is, in itself; it is unconditioned.

It exists as a continuum—regardless of sensory phenomena or perception.

While space as a mental construct exists by way of spatial extensions and relationships, space, in itself, is a continuum that is unconditioned, unbounded, and infinite—with neither a beginning nor an ending.

Space transcends all physical attributes.

Space, the Source and Culmination of All Things
69

Space is the source and culmination of all things in the universe.

The three natures of our universe—physical, physiological, and psychological—are intrinsically held in the domain of all-pervading space.

Space preserves the individuality of all things concrete and abstract—from the infinitesimal to the infinite.

Every fiber of every substance that pertains to finite nature is infiltrated and surrounded by space.

Space encompasses the three times—as the past, the present, and the future.

Space is devoid of physical attributes.

Space, the Ground
of Empty Essence
70

Space is the subtlest level of wondrous nature.

It may also be described as openness or emptiness—though abundant with pure essence for all possibilities to arise.

Space is analogous to consciousness, in an ultimate sense—as the great seal called MIND that encompasses all things both terrestrial and celestial.

Space,
of Undifferentiated LOVE
71

Space is the mother or ground for all of being—to arise, to prevail, to decline, and to dissolve.

It is the field of all possibilities—as the womb of all phenomena.

It is 'the unconditioned' and 'the infinite'.

It is undifferentiated LOVE.

Space, All-Embracing
72

Space is the field of transcendence; its nature is immutable.

Space is MIND, or cosmic consciousness, itself.

Space surrounds, infiltrates, and penetrates all of matter and mental phenomena.

Space, Ultimate!
73

Space is the ultimate nature of the universe; it is a dimensionless, beginningless, and endless continuum—as 'one whole'.

It surpasses all mental constructs or physical attributes.

However, it is the play-field of all phenomenal or conventional realities—in terms of synthesized life-experience!

Space Epitomizes
Wisdom and Compassion
74

Space is the ultimate wisdom and compassion epitomized.

It is the all-pervading wisdom of emptiness and openness coupled with luminous compassion—as LOVE in action—that sees through the eyes of all beings and forms.

Space embodies luminous essence of infinite potential; it resonates the presence of the GREAT MYSTERIOUS VOID that mirrors the psychedelic sensory experiences, called phenomena, or LIFE.

Space Beholds Relativity
75

Space makes spatial extensions—as sensory objects in the field of relativity—possible.

Without space, could **our three-tiered universe** of—coarse (matter), subtle (energy), and secret (essence)—exist?

Without space, could **our universe of three natures** exist?

- as an imagined and projected field of representations and imputations

- as a field of causal processes effected through interdependent co-emergence of phenomena

- as a perfected, undifferentiated reality of 'suchness'—through self-realization

In the absence of space would **the three times— past, present, or future**—exist?

Space in Time; Time in Space
76

The concept of time—as past, present, and future—is embedded in space.

Space and time—as conventional constructs of mind—are merely two faces of one reality.

Time exists because of space; space exists because of time.

Space embodies the indivisible, inseparable, interdependent trinity of 'being and form'—at the coarse, subtle, and very subtle, or secret, levels of being—through eternity.

Time encompasses the illusory spatial extensions of history and mystery, called past and future.

Space
Analogous to Consciousness
77

Space, to emphasize, is synonymous with consciousness.

It epitomizes both the absolute and relative truths as two dimensions of one LOVE; these two aspects are analogous to the wave effect and particle effect of the electromagnetic spectrum of phenomena.

Differently expressed, the wave effect is the unbound, unconditioned, and undifferentiated.

The particle effect is the momentary appearance and disappearance of luminosity—contingent upon observation alone.

Space, Infinite, Symbolized
78

Space signifies infinity.

The geometric shape of a point—elaborated upon with a zero—is symbolic of limitless, unfathomable space, neither with beginning, nor with ending.

This point that transcends dimensions—by way of space and time—is envisioned as the seed syllable of infinite vibration, in accordance with ancient wisdom.

The color blue denotes space.

Space,
as a Sensory Perception
79

Space gives rise to the sense of hearing.

All vibrations of universal being, of body-speech-mind, merge in space into one infinite hum—'OM'—the seed syllable of infinite vibration.

OM integrates all cries of existence—as the 'sorrows and lamentations' and 'joys and rejoices' of LIFE.

Nelunika Gunawardena Rajapakse

Nature's Four Wondrous Energies

Photo credit: www.publicdomainpictures.net

Appreciating the Four Wondrous Energies or Abstract Elements that Compose Life and Being!

Gratitude to Mother Earth
80

"Thank you, Mother Earth—our ground of being!"

"We feel your solidity, security, dependability, and stability beneath our feet—as we stand, we walk, we run, and we leap!"

"You are the source and culmination of comfort—as we rest, we lie, we dream, and we sleep!"

"You are the incubator, nourisher, and nurturer—abounded with creativity, charity, forgiveness, resilience and LOVE, unconditional."

"Above all, you are feminine LOVE—suffused with fertility, prosperity, balance, and abundance."

"You are the epitome of passive intuition—of wisdom-compassion!"

Gratitude to Water, Life-Beholder
81

"Thank you, Water—life-beholder—of introspective maternal LOVE."

"We feel your presence through every crack and pore of Earth, as cleanser, cooler, clarifier, pacifier, and embracer."

"You are the purifier, healer, receiver (of all pains), and life-generator—of strength, fluidity, fertility, and all-encompassing devotion!"

"You are wisdom-compassion, sole life-sustainer!"

Gratitude to Fire,
of Wondrous Love
82

"Thank you, Fire—of wondrous LOVE—you are energy at work to incubate, to generate, to purify, and to transmute all passions of life, as world in flux!"

Gratitude to Air,
Of Uncompromising LOVE
83

"Thank you, Swift Air—of uncompromising wisdom-compassion—you are the fresh breath of life that weaves through all finite things, ephemeral!"

Gratitude to Space, Great Mother
84

"Thank you, Great Mother Space—the womb, of all phenomena—for the 'dance of life' no mistake!"

"You are vast, you are deep, your unfathomable emptiness is the very essence—luminous—indeed!"

Nature, the Wonder
85

Nature is the Wonder of Existence and Non-existence manifested by the union of four wondrous aggregate material energies! These are the abstract energies of which the universe is constituted.

Each of them bears two seemingly apparent converse characteristics—although, on close examination, they are found to be the same.

Abstract Earth—to harden, and to soften—of resistance

Abstract Water—to flow, and to paste—of cohesion

Abstract Air—to expand, and to contract—of motion

Abstract Fire—to heat, and to cool—of transmutation

Universal Energies
as Units of Action
86

Essentially, the four types of abstract universal energies are units of action that exist by repetition.

They are the basic energies that underlie the common substances known—as earth, water, air, and fire.

The four principle energies, together, coalesce—in different proportions—to create substances. No substance in the universe is formed without the embrace of all four energies.

Every substance, in consequence, bears the eight characteristics (as mentioned on the previous page) in diverse proportions.

The features of every substance formed, is the very presence of the four abstract energies—in terms of their proportional representation—and their associated eight characteristics.

Our World of Substances
87

There are over one hundred known basic chemical elements or substances in the universe; they cannot be broken down or inter-converted into simpler substances; these are conventionally looked upon as the primary constituents of matter.

Each chemical element is, therefore, distinguished by its atomic number that denotes the number of protons in the nuclei of its atoms.

The elements assume the solid, liquid, gaseous, or plasma states of matter, contingent upon the union of the four energies proportionately combined—by way of units, and their multiples—of earth (of resistance), water (of cohesion), air (of motion), and fire (of transmutation).

Four Aggregate Energies
88

Aggregate energies of matter, as have been clearly understood by now, are composed of each other.

All known and unknown substances in the universe are formed by the essential union of these four sublime energies—in the form of different combinations and proportions.

Whether a substance is more solid, more liquid, more gaseous, or plasma, is contingent upon the nature of its material properties—in terms of their combinations and proportions.

Since our material universe is composed of substances that have come about by the indispensable union of the four aggregate energies, its ultimate destruction is the very dissolution of the world of substances.

However, the abstract energies that constitute the substances will never be destroyed; they are indestructible and infinite.

Rigid, Cohesive, Dispersive and Combustive Nature
89

If the combination contains more units of the abstract energy of resistance, the substance will bear the nature of solidity.

If the combination contains more units of the abstract energy of cohesion, the substance will bear the nature of fluidity.

If the combination contains more units of the abstract energy of dispersion, the substance will assume a gaseous nature.

If a major portion of the combination contains units of the abstract energy of transmutation, the substance will bear a combustive nature.

Nature,
Our Sentient Experience
90

Nature, whether we agree, or not, is the universe of sentient experience brought forth by the incessant interactions of the four wondrous energies—of resistance (abstract earth), cohesion (abstract water), motion (abstract air), and transmutation (abstract fire) infiltrated by space, all pervasive!

The four abstract energies are discernible to the mind alone, until and unless, they unite to bring about our world of substances.

Their natures are, consequently, discernible to the senses, only through the medium of substances—as earth, water, air, and fire.

Nature, Ultimate
91

Nature, in an ultimate sense, is a phenomenological manifestation implying that it is based on direct sensory experience—through the medium of substances.

The four basic elements—earth, water, fire, and air—being aggregates of each other, are the primary forces that interactively sustain LIFE, as we know. Accordingly, the physical/physiological/psychological universes of matter and energy are governed by these four aggregate elements.

Maintaining equilibrium or balance between the four operative forces—with regard to the mind and its associated instrumental world—is pivotal towards overall physical, physiological, and psychological well-being.

Phenomenology of Sensory Experience
92

The phenomenology of sensory experience provides a synthesized presentation of events in life as 'the here' and 'the now' within a vast and supreme web of co-emergent interdependencies—from the infinitesimal to the infinite!

In this scheme of existence—of incessant possibilities—our sentient experience is a projection and a product of psychophysical 'electromagnetic vibrations of energy at interplay' in the supremely expansive and unconditioned VOID, called space—that is the space of MIND!

Afterword
93

Thank you, dear readers, for your time well spent to deeply understand our place in nature. We are in it together, transcending all labels and imputations of convention placed upon objects of mind.

By now, I do hope that you realize that everything is nature; and nature is the marvelous display—of the great union—of four abstract, wondrous, and infinite, material energies coalescing and dancing in space, supremely and magnanimously as multitudinous name, form, and being.

They assemble and disassemble, unceasingly, to form our world of substances. Their incessant interplay—to bring forth atomic and molecular patterns of energy—is 'the marvelous magic show' of the cosmos we know, by means of our senses, called sensory perception.

Afterword—2

We all are witnesses to the great cosmic ballet of the substances that display the sublime energies of resistance, cohesion, transmutation, and motion infiltrated and pervaded by space—the womb of infinite possibilities!

We, together, are participants in this dance of wondrous energy—as constellations of energy, at a subtle level, or perhaps, constitutions of physical/physiological processes, at a coarse level!

From a psychological vantage point, our vibrations of energy in the great cosmic expression intrinsically possess the power and potency—both individually and collectively—to refine the dance, or even not!

Be that as it may, the deep-seated and sublime inmost force of mind—as the progenitor of higher realization—bears the essence to transform how things manifest by the energy of COMPASSION we invest upon it!

So let us be grateful for what we have, today, and return our LOVE to make our world a better place to live, each day—by the choices we make in body, speech, and mind!

About the Author
94

Nelunika Gunawardena Rajapakse is a proud citizen of her world having been long in residence—nearly five decades—in the United States.

She is the only daughter, besides two precious sons, of the late Dionicious and Mildred Gunawardena, who arrived in the USA, in the mid-1960's. The latter was trained directly under Dr. Maria Montessori in 1943, and it was her pride and joy to share the original version of Montessori, amidst a growing interest, then, in the United States—to assimilate and put into practice its innovative educational principles.

Nelunika, needless to say, has been a product of this unmatched authentic vision from the very inception of her life, to this day—naturally equipped to nurture, inspire, and educate, children of humanity (from birth through adolescence, and beyond), grounded in morally sensitive awareness.

About the Author—2

Mentored all along by her resolutely dedicated Montessori pedagogue mother—and, together, having worked in partnership for three decades— Nelunika is a proud beneficiary of an experientially founded, intellectual legacy. She boasts a rich, cumulative history of exemplary Montessori in practice for over forty years, having been the head directress, administrator, and chief operating officer of the much admired Bainbridge~Solon Montessori School (1970-2012) that served scores of children and parents in Ohio, USA.

The author, above and beyond all things, cherishes her morally grounded 'lived and learned' upbringing under the nurturing guidance of her parents.

About the Author—3

Nelunika's life idols, accordingly, are her parents who epitomized, through every breath of their existence, the compassionate values that remain central and universal to the great scheme called 'existence'. In observation of this view, all things, indeed, possess intrinsic richness; they call for equal value and respect—shunning egocentric norms, labels, and attitudes.

Nelunika, in turn, reflects on living a spiritually rich life through every breath of her own existence. She realizes that improvement and enrichment in sustaining values 'as a help to life'—to all that compose life—requires patience and mindful effort, hand in hand. Hence, maintaining a selfless cultivated awareness is crucial to life's overall success. The aspiration to guide others in the direction of true peace and eternal joy, thus, is Nelunika's heartfelt wish.

About the Author—4

Presently, the author lives her renewed and pioneering vision along her steadfast mission to 'Raise the Position of Today's Child and the World' while sharing her 'Vision for Intellectual Wellness for all Ages'. As such, she disseminates her wisdom and expertise through the creation of invaluable time-stamps of her life-experience.

In this day and age of confused human values and ideals, Nelunika stands passionately upon her convictions—to improve the human condition by way of books, videos, blogs, and dedicated websites.

Additionally, Nelunika Gunawardena Rajapakse is a devoted professional trainer, and a mentor for parents—engaged in sharing her expertise by way of lectures, seminars, consultations, and continuous guidance to organizations, schools, individuals, and diverse social groups.

About the Author—5

She is the author of ten books:

1. Compassionate Engaged Parenting as a Help to Life

2. Parenting as a Help to Life

3. Roots of Moral Sensitivity and the Emerging Tree of Life

4. The Active Brain—A Vision for Intellectual Wellness—Book 1

5. The Active Brain—A Vision for Intellectual Wellness—Book 2 Volume 1

6. The Active Brain—A Vision for Intellectual Wellness—Book 2 Volume 2

7. Healing Breath the Wind of Life
    (A Seeds of Wisdom Presentation—Book 1)

8. Rhythm of Nature, the Rhythm of Life!
    (A Seeds of Wisdom Presentation—Book 2)

9. Reflections Upon the Mirror of MIND (forthcoming)
    (A Seeds of Wisdom Presentation—Book 3)

10. Nature is Everything
    (A 'Seeds of Wisdom for the Maturing Intellect' Presentation for Children—Book 1)

11. Nature is Everything
    (A 'Seeds of Wisdom for the Maturing Intellect' Presentation for Children—Book 2)

Acknowledgement
95

My heartfelt gratitude goes to Debra Murray who has remained beside me to offer her gracious moral and technical support through the many pages of this book.

www.ingramcontent.com/pod-product-compliance
Lightning Source LLC
Chambersburg PA
CBHW020536290526
45786CB00002B/914